CHEMISTRY
YOU CAN CHOMP

JESSIE ALKIRE

Consulting Editor, Diane Craig, MA/Reading Specialist

Super Sandcastle

An Imprint of Abdo Publishing
abdobooks.com

ABDOBOOKS.COM

Published by Abdo Publishing, a division of ABDO, PO Box 398166, Minneapolis, Minnesota 55439. Copyright © 2019 by Abdo Consulting Group, Inc. International copyrights reserved in all countries. No part of this book may be reproduced in any form without written permission from the publisher. Super SandCastle™ is a trademark and logo of Abdo Publishing.

Printed in the United States of America, North Mankato, Minnesota
102018
012019

 THIS BOOK CONTAINS RECYCLED MATERIALS

Design: Emily O'Malley, Mighty Media, Inc.
Production: Mighty Media, Inc.
Editor: Liz Salzmann
Cover Photographs: Mighty Media, Inc.; Shutterstock
Interior Photographs: Mighty Media, Inc.; Shutterstock; Wellcome Collection

The following manufacturers/names appearing in this book are trademarks: Argo®, Arm & Hammer™, C&H®, Clear Value®, Essential Everyday®, Gold Emblem™, Knox®, Morton®, Old Home®, Pyrex®, Reynolds®, Cut-Rite®, Skittles®, Target®

Library of Congress Control Number: 2018948855

Publisher's Cataloging-in-Publication Data
Names: Alkire, Jessie, author.
Title: Chemistry you can chomp / by Jessie Alkire.
Description: Minneapolis, Minnesota : Abdo Publishing, 2019 | Series: Super simple science you can snack on
Identifiers: ISBN 9781532117237 (lib. bdg.) | ISBN 9781532170096 (ebook)
Subjects: LCSH: Chemistry--Juvenile literature. | Cooking--Juvenile literature. | Science--Experiments--Juvenile literature. | Gastronomy--Juvenile literature.
Classification: DDC 641.0--dc23

Super SandCastle™ books are created by a team of professional educators, reading specialists, and content developers around five essential components—phonemic awareness, phonics, vocabulary, text comprehension, and fluency—to assist young readers as they develop reading skills and strategies and increase their general knowledge. All books are written, reviewed, and leveled for guided reading and early reading intervention programs for use in shared, guided, and independent reading and writing activities to support a balanced approach to literacy instruction.

TO ADULT HELPERS

The projects in this book are fun and simple. There are just a few things to remember to keep kids safe. Some projects require the use of sharp or hot objects. Also, kids may be using messy ingredients. Make sure they protect their clothes and work surfaces. Review the projects before starting, and be ready to assist when necessary.

KEY SYMBOLS

Watch for these warning symbols in this book. Here is what they mean.

HOT!
You will be working with something hot. Get help!

SHARP!
You will be working with something sharp. Get help!

CONTENTS

WHAT IS CHEMISTRY?

Chemistry is the study of matter. All matter is made of atoms. The center of an atom is the nucleus. The nucleus contains **protons** and **neutrons**. Electrons move around the nucleus.

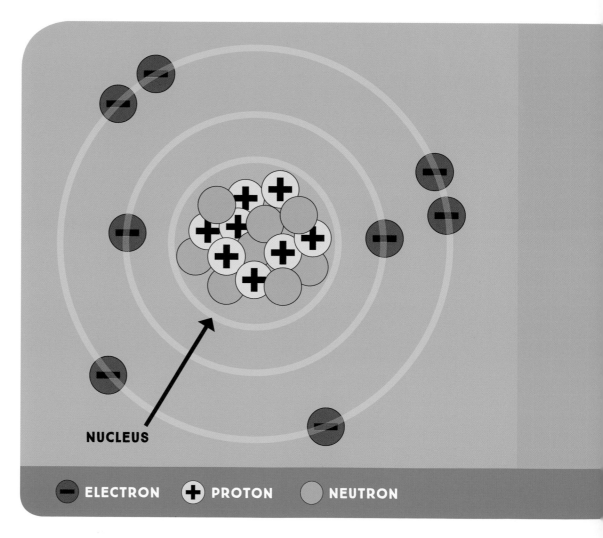

NUCLEUS

ELECTRON   PROTON   NEUTRON

IRISH SCIENTIST ROBERT BOYLE IS OFTEN CALLED THE FIRST MODERN CHEMIST. HE LIVED IN THE 1600S.

Chemists are scientists who study the properties of matter. They also study how different types of matter and energy **react** to each other.

Chemical reactions occur around us every day. They happen in everything from cooking to medicine. Studying chemistry can help us understand our world and the things in it.

Today, chemistry is important to many **industries**. These include energy, entertainment, and health care. Here are examples of the way chemistry is used in each of these industries.

NUCLEAR FISSION

Nuclear fission is the process of breaking a nucleus apart. This creates nuclear energy. Nuclear energy can power and heat homes and businesses!

NUCLEAR POWER IS CREATED IN LARGE POWER PLANTS.

LCD SCREENS

LCD stands for liquid crystal display. LCD screens are used in televisions, cell phones, and more. In an LCD, electricity is applied to liquid crystals. The electric current changes the colors shown on the screen.

LCD SCREENS COME IN MANY SIZES.

3-D PRINTING

3-D printers can print 3-D objects. Scientists use chemistry to create the plastic and other **substances** used by 3-D printers to make objects.

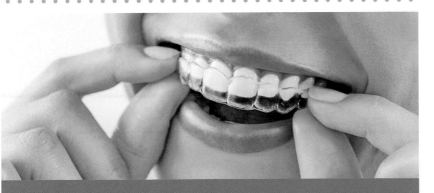

DENTISTS CAN USE 3-D PRINTERS TO MAKE CLEAR BRACES FOR STRAIGHTENING TEETH.

CHEMISTRY SNACKS

You can learn a lot about chemistry by making the fun snacks in this book!

GET READY

* Ask an adult for **permission** to use kitchen tools and ingredients.

* Read the snack's list of tools and ingredients. Make sure you have everything you need.

* Does a snack require ingredients you don't like? Get creative! Find other ingredients you enjoy instead.

SNACK CLEAN & SAFE

* Clean your work surface before you start.

* Wash your hands before you work with food.

* Keep your work area tidy. This makes it easier to find what you need.

* Ask an adult for help when handling sharp or hot objects.

CLEANING UP

* Don't waste unused ingredients! Store leftover ingredients to use later.

* Clean your work surface. Wash any dishes or tools you used.

* Wash your hands before you eat your snack!

INGREDIENTS & TOOLS

BAKING SODA

CORNSTARCH

GUMMY BEARS

HOT CHOCOLATE PACKETS

LEMONS

LIGHT CORN SYRUP

PEPPERONI SLICES

POWDERED SUGAR

PREMADE PIZZA CRUST

SHREDDED MOZZARELLA CHEESE

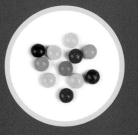

SKITTLES CANDIES

SLICED MUSHROOMS

TOMATO SAUCE

UNFLAVORED GELATIN

VANILLA

HERE ARE SOME OF THE INGREDIENTS AND TOOLS YOU WILL NEED TO MAKE THE SNACKS IN THIS BOOK.

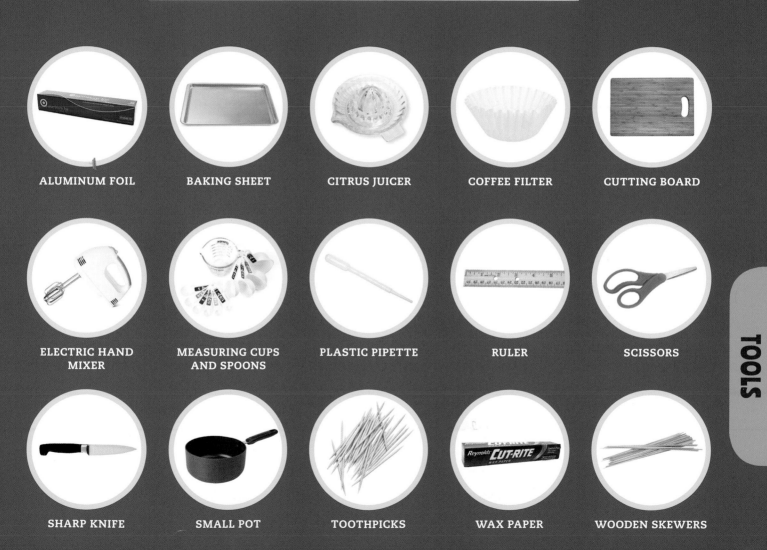

ALUMINUM FOIL	BAKING SHEET	CITRUS JUICER	COFFEE FILTER	CUTTING BOARD
ELECTRIC HAND MIXER	MEASURING CUPS AND SPOONS	PLASTIC PIPETTE	RULER	SCISSORS
SHARP KNIFE	SMALL POT	TOOTHPICKS	WAX PAPER	WOODEN SKEWERS

TOOLS

ATOMIC PIZZA

INGREDIENTS

- premade pizza crust
- tomato sauce
- shredded mozzarella cheese
- pepperoni slices
- sliced mushrooms
- green & black olives

TOOLS

- spoon
- baking sheet
- oven mitts

You learned about atoms on page 4. Now try making a model of an atom by baking a yummy pizza!

1. Lay the pizza crust on your work surface. Cover the crust with tomato sauce.

2. Sprinkle cheese on top of the sauce. Place pepperoni around the edge of the pizza.

3. Create a smaller circle of pepperoni in the middle of the pizza. This is the nucleus.

4. Place four mushroom slices on the large pepperoni circle. Place two mushroom slices on the small pepperoni circle. The mushrooms are electrons.

5. Place six green olives and six black olives in the middle of the small circle. These are **protons** and **neutrons**.

6. Place the pizza on the baking sheet. Have an adult help you bake the pizza. Follow the instructions on the pizza crust package. Let the pizza cool. Observe your atomic pizza before digging in!

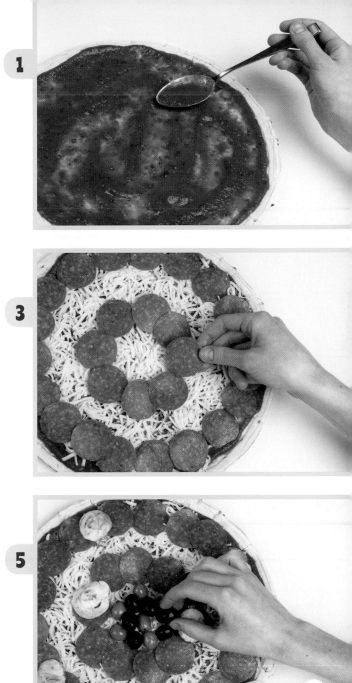

HOT CHOCOLATE SOLUTION 🔥

INGREDIENTS

- water
- 3 hot chocolate packets

TOOLS

- 3 mugs
- liquid measuring cup
- 3 spoons
- stopwatch (optional)

Dissolving a powder in a liquid creates a **solution**. The temperature of the liquid can affect how well something dissolves in it. Experiment with solutions by making hot chocolate!

1. Pour 1 cup of cold water into the first mug.

2. Pour 1 cup of room temperature tap water into the second mug.

3. Pour 1 cup of room temperature tap water into the third mug. Microwave it for 90 seconds.

4. Add a packet of hot chocolate mix to each mug.

5. Have a friend or two help you stir the three solutions until the powder dissolves. Which was the first to dissolve completely? Try using a stopwatch to time them.

6. Enjoy your hot chocolate!

FIZZING LEMONADE

INGREDIENTS

- 2 lemons
- baking soda
- water
- sugar

TOOLS

- sharp knife
- cutting board
- citrus juicer
- liquid measuring cup
- paper
- pencil
- strainer
- drinking glass
- measuring spoons
- spoon

One type of chemical **reaction** is an acid-base reaction. Lemon juice is an acid. Baking soda is a base. Combining them produces bubbles! You can see this reaction by making **fizzy** lemonade!

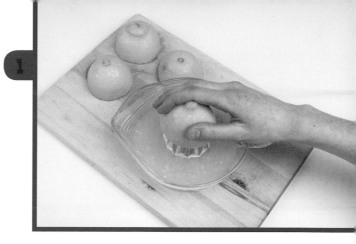

1. Have an adult help you cut the lemons in half. Use the citrus juicer to juice the lemons.

2. Pour the lemon juice into the measuring cup. Write down how much juice you produced.

3. Place the strainer over the drinking glass. Pour the juice through the strainer into the glass. Remove the strainer.

4. Add a teaspoon of baking soda to the lemon juice. Watch it fizz!

5. Measure water equal to the amount of lemon juice you measured in step 2. Add 1 to 2 teaspoons of sugar to the water. Stir until the sugar is **dissolved**.

6. Add the sugar mixture to the lemon juice.

7. Take a sip of lemonade! How does it taste? How does the lemonade feel in your mouth?

ENDOTHERMIC SLUSHY

INGREDIENTS
- juice
- ice
- coarse salt

TOOLS
- plastic cup
- large bowl
- wooden skewer

Some chemical **reactions** make **substances** colder. These are **endothermic** reactions. Try using salt and ice to create a cold, sweet treat!

1. Fill the plastic cup with juice. Place the cup in the large bowl.

2. Fill the bowl with ice. The ice should cover the cup up to the level of the juice.

3. Sprinkle salt over the ice until the ice is coated. Be careful not to get any salt in the juice!

4. Leave the juice in the bowl of ice for several hours. Stir the juice with the wooden skewer every 30 minutes. How does the juice change?

5. After 1 to 2 hours, the juice should start to freeze. Keep stirring it regularly. This allows it to thicken into **slush** without freezing completely.

6. Once it is as thick as you like it, taste your fruit **slushy**!

MARSHMALLOW MAGIC

INGREDIENTS

- non-stick cooking spray
- ⅓ cup cornstarch
- ⅓ cup powdered sugar
- 2 packets of unflavored gelatin
- ½ cup cold water
- 1 cup light corn syrup
- ½ cup sugar
- ½ teaspoon vanilla

TOOLS

- 8 × 8-inch baking pan
- wax paper
- scissors
- mixing bowls
- measuring cups & spoons
- spoon
- small pot
- electric hand mixer
- spatula
- cutting board
- sharp knife

Matter exists in three main states. These are gas, liquid, and solid. You can see matter change between solid and liquid by making marshmallows!

1. Coat the baking pan with non-stick cooking spray.

2. Cut a piece of wax paper to fit the bottom of the pan. Place the wax paper in the pan. Coat the wax paper with non-stick cooking spray.

3. Stir the cornstarch and powdered sugar together in a small bowl.

4. Put some of the cornstarch mixture on the wax paper in the pan. **Tilt** the pan in all directions to spread the mixture to all sides of the pan. Pour any loose cornstarch mixture back into the small bowl. Set the pan aside.

5. Put the gelatin in a small pot. Add the water. Wait one minute.

6. Set the pot on a stove burner. Have an adult help you heat the pot on low until the gelatin is **dissolved**. Take the pot off the burner. Set it aside.

Continued on the next page.

8

7. Put the corn syrup, sugar, and vanilla in a large bowl. Add the gelatin mixture to the corn syrup mixture.

8. Have an adult help you use the electric hand mixer to **blend** the mixture for 15 minutes. It should become thick and creamy.

9. Pour the mixture into the baking pan. Use the spatula to spread it out evenly. Let the mixture sit for at least four hours.

10

10. Spread some of the cornstarch mixture on a cutting board. Turn the baking pan upside down on the cutting board. Lift the pan off of the marshmallow sheet.

11. Peel the wax paper from the top of the marshmallow sheet.

12. Dip a knife in hot tap water. Have an adult help you cut the marshmallow sheet into small squares. Dip the knife in hot water again if marshmallow gets stuck to the knife.

13

13. Sprinkle the remaining cornstarch mixture over the marshmallows. This keeps them from sticking together. Enjoy your homemade marshmallows!

SCIENCE BITE

GAS   LIQUID   SOLID

IN WATER, GELATIN'S MOLECULES SPREAD OUT. HEAT BREAKS DOWN THEIR BONDS. THE GELATIN DISSOLVES. IT BECOMES PART OF THE LIQUID. AS THE GELATIN COOLS, ITS MOLECULES' BONDS REFORM. THE GELATIN BECOMES SOLID AGAIN.

THE SAME PROCESS CAUSES WATER TO CHANGE ITS STATE. WHEN WATER BOILS, IT TURNS INTO A GAS, OR STEAM. WHEN STEAM COOLS, THE GAS TURNS BACK INTO LIQUID. WHEN WATER FREEZES INTO ICE, IT BECOMES A SOLID.

OSMOSIS GUMMY BEARS ⬤

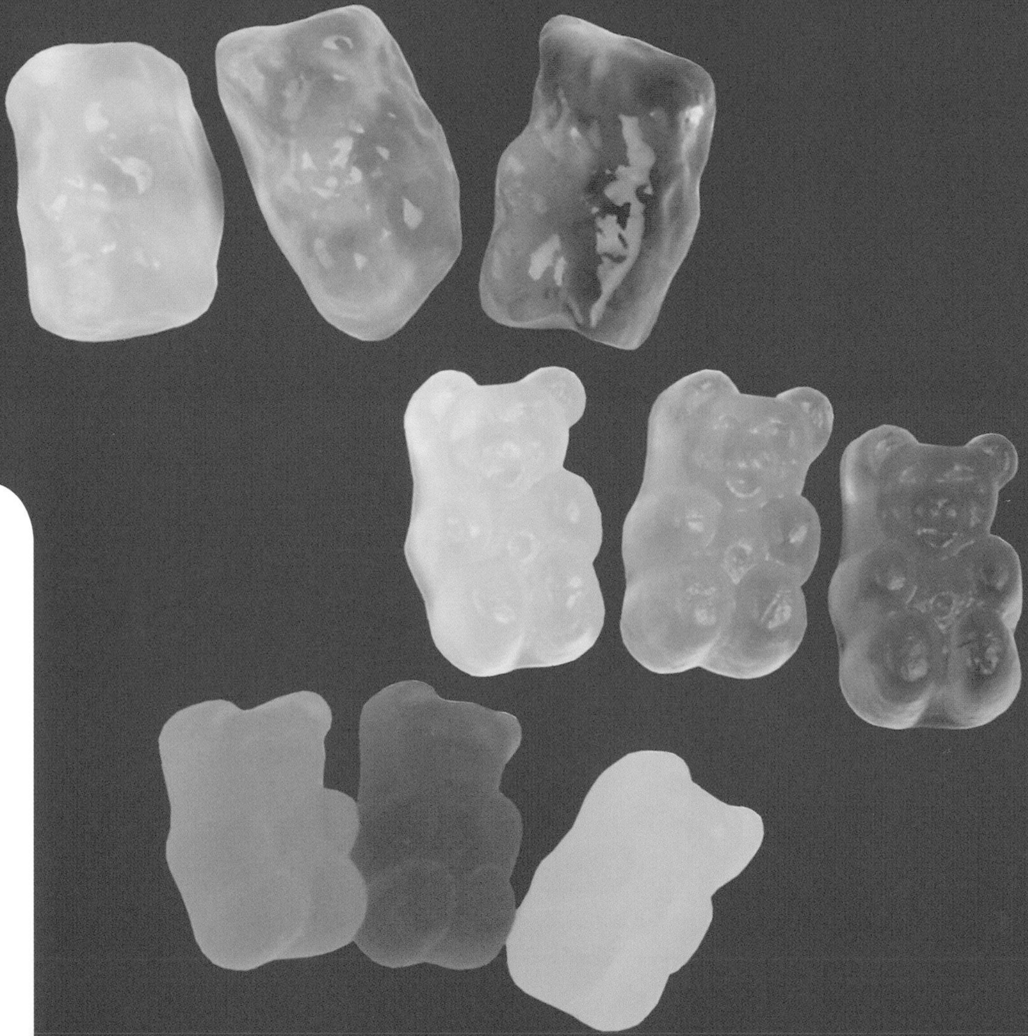

INGREDIENTS

- water
- salt
- gummy bears

TOOLS

- liquid measuring cup
- large bowl
- spoon
- 3 small bowls

Osmosis is a process that causes a liquid to move into a solid **substance**. You can see osmosis at work by placing gummy bears in salt water!

1. Have an adult help you boil 2 cups of water. Pour the water into the large bowl.

2. Stir salt into the water until no more salt will **dissolve**.

3. Put the bowl of salt water in the refrigerator for about 30 minutes.

4. Place some gummy bears in each small bowl.

5. Pour the salt water into one bowl.

6. Pour 2 cups of plain water into the second bowl. Add no water to the third bowl.

7. Label the bowl of salt water so you remember which one it is.

8. Let the gummy bears sit for at least three hours. How did the gummy bears change? Which type of water caused the most change?

9. Throw out the saltwater gummy bears. Eat the other gummy bears for a snack!

CANDY CHROMATOGRAPHY

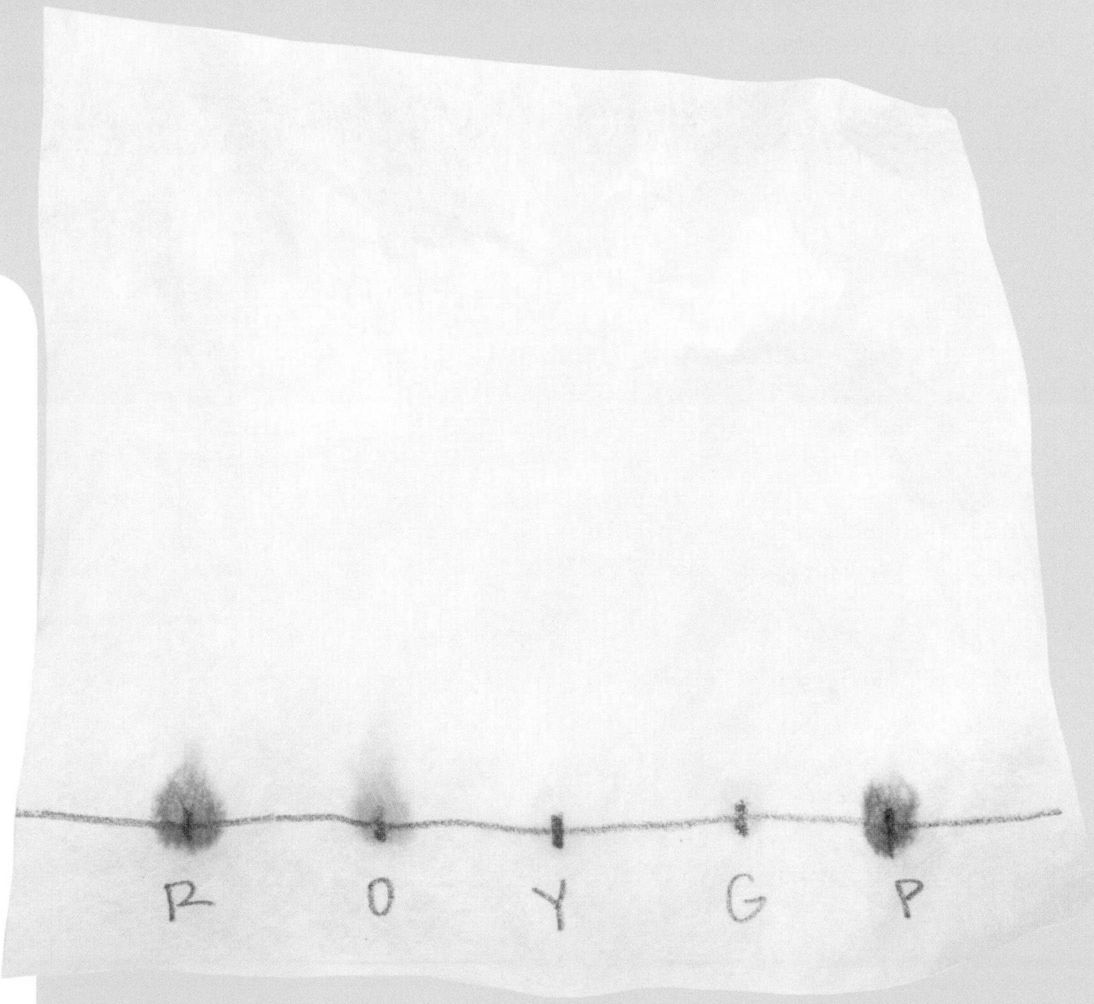

INGREDIENTS

- Skittles
- water
- salt

TOOLS

- aluminum foil
- ruler
- plastic pipette
- coffee filter
- scissors
- pencil
- toothpick
- measuring cup & spoons
- small bowl

Chromatography is a way to separate parts of a mixture. In chromatography, the mixture is passed through a **medium**. One medium is filter paper. Try chromatography with Skittles and water!

1. Place one of each color of Skittles on a piece of foil. Space them about 1 inch (2.5 cm) apart.

2. Use the pipette to put a drop of water next to a Skittle. Move the Skittle onto the water. Repeat for the other Skittles.

3. Let the Skittles sit in the water drops until the water turns the color of the Skittles.

4. Cut a square out of the middle of the coffee filter.

5. Use a ruler and pencil to draw a line near the bottom of the square.

6. Draw five evenly spaced marks along the line. Label each mark with the first letter of a Skittle color.

Continued on the next page.

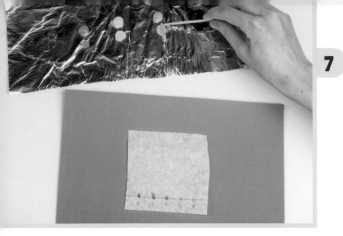

7

12

13

7. Use a toothpick to pick up a droplet of colored water. Place the droplet on the mark for that color. Repeat with the other colors. Try to keep the droplets as small as possible.

8. Let the droplets dry.

9. Repeat steps 7 and 8 two more times.

10. Measure 1 cup of hot tap water. Stir in ⅛ teaspoon salt until it is completely **dissolved**.

11. Pour salt water into the bowl until it is about 1 inch (2.5 cm) deep.

12. Hold the bottom edge of the coffee filter in the salt water. Don't let the water touch the colored droplets.

13. As the salt water passes through the filter, the colored drops should start to spread. Remove the paper when the salt water nears the top of the filter. Let the filter dry.

14. Study the filter. Which colors spread farthest? Don't forget to eat the Skittles!

SCIENCE BITE

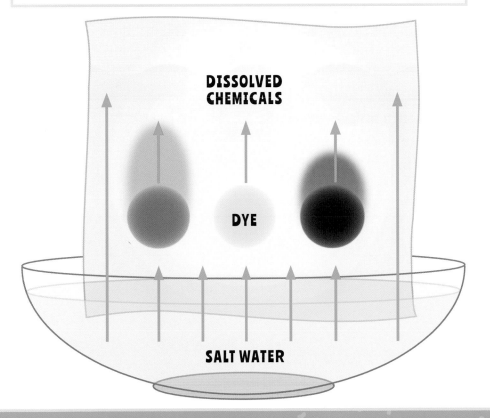

DISSOLVED
CHEMICALS

DYE

SALT WATER

THE SALT WATER MOVES UP THE FILTER PAPER. WHEN IT REACHES THE
DOTS OF DYE, THE CHEMICALS IN THE DYES START TO DISSOLVE. THESE
CHEMICALS MOVE UP THE FILTER WITH THE WATER. THE CHEMICALS IN
SOME DYES TRAVEL FARTHER THAN OTHERS. THE WATER KEEPS GOING.
THIS SEPARATES THE CHEMICALS FROM THE WATER.

CONCLUSION

Chemistry is the study of matter and how it behaves. This includes combining and separating **substances** to create chemical **reactions**. Chemists are people who study chemistry. Chemists can help us understand the world.

MAKING SNACKS IS JUST ONE WAY TO LEARN ABOUT CHEMISTRY. HOW WILL YOU CONTINUE YOUR CHEMISTRY ADVENTURE?

QUIZ

1. **ALL MATTER IS MADE OF ATOMS.** TRUE OR FALSE?

2. **WHAT IS THE PROCESS OF BREAKING A NUCLEUS APART CALLED?**

3. **HOW MANY MAIN STATES OF MATTER ARE THERE?**

LEARN MORE ABOUT IT!

YOU CAN FIND OUT MORE ABOUT CHEMISTRY AT THE LIBRARY. OR YOU CAN ASK AN ADULT TO HELP YOU FIND INFORMATION ABOUT CHEMISTRY ON THE INTERNET!

ANSWERS: 1. TRUE   2. NUCLEAR FISSION   3. THREE

GLOSSARY

blend – to mix together so that you can't tell one ingredient from another.

dissolve – to mix with a liquid so that it becomes part of the liquid.

endothermic – related to or formed by taking in heat.

fizz – to create a lot of tiny hissing bubbles. Something that has hissing bubbles is fizzy.

industry – the process of using machines and factories to make products.

medium – a substance through which something passes or is carried, such as air.

molecule – a group of two or more atoms that make up the smallest piece of a substance.

neutron (NOO-trahn) – a particle in an atom's nucleus with a neutral charge.

permission – when a person in charge says it's okay to do something.

proton – a particle in an atom's nucleus with a positive charge.

react – to change when mixed with another chemical or substance. Such a change is a reaction.

slush – something that is part ice and part liquid, such as melting snow.

slushy – a thick, partly frozen drink usually made with ice and juice or fruit.

solution – a liquid in which something has been dissolved.

substance – anything that takes up space, such as a solid object or a liquid.

tilt – to make something lean or tip to the side.